The Way Fourth

The Way Fourth

Poems by

Peter Waldor

© 2025 Peter Waldor. All rights reserved.
This material may not be reproduced in any form, published,
reprinted, recorded, performed, broadcast,
rewritten or redistributed without
the explicit permission of Peter Waldor.
All such actions are strictly prohibited by law.

Cover design by Shay Culligan
Cover image by Peter Waldor
Author photo by Gabriel Waldor
Mountains illustration by Annie Spratt on Unsplash

ISBN: 978-1-63980-822-9

Kelsay Books
502 South 1040 East, A-119
American Fork, Utah 84003
Kelsaybooks.com

for Lisa, again and again

Other Books by Peter Waldor

Door to a Noisy Room
The Wilderness Poetry of Wu Xing
Who Touches Everything
The Unattended Harp
State of the Union
Gate Posts with No Gate
Nice Dumpling
Owl Gulch Elegies
Unmade Friend
Something About the Way
The Way 2
Midwife vs Obstetrician
Hats Off
Seven Quilts (essays)
Snowy Saplings
Understandings and Misunderstandings
At the Next Table
Time Can't Tell It's Being Told
Beginning Polyamory
Fairy Slippers
wellwhadayasay?
Turnstiles
14 Meditation Prompts and a Treatise on Noble Silence
The Third Way
You Alone Know
Tapadawhirld
Immigration Is the Essence of Democracy
Intermediate Polyamory
One Can NEVER Predict the Past

Contents

X

Radical	15
Tree Hugger	16
The Palace of Wisdom	18
The Hummingbird's Tongue	21
To Textile Manufacturers	22
Bad Timing	24
When I Return	25
It All Feels Good	26
The Most Peaceful Day	27
My Higher Self	28
Doing the Dishes	29
With My Love After the Symphony	30
Trophy	33
Smell	35
Osha	36

X

On and Off	41
Time Constraints	43
Hierarchy	44
Makeup	45
Calling Names	47
Wishbone	48
My Love	50
Of the Americas	52
Happy Birthday!	54
Breakfast	55

Yawn	56
The Right Mirror	57
True Love	59

X

Silk Bag	67
A Great Hula Hooper	68
Ridicule	69
Go Low	70
Lies	71
Alarming	72
Cool Hands	73
Glitter and Ashes	74
Uncovering	75
Kept Ribbon	76
Balm Jar	77
Shook	78
Preparing	79
Bodies	80
The Order of Oral Sex	81
Seven Beaches in a Day	82
Branch	83

X

Radical

Years ago
you delayed
cutting the cords
and the hospital
nurses refused
to care for the
babies because
you wouldn't
follow their
procedure and
then you returned
a few years later
and that was the
standard of care-
delaying cutting
the cord.
If only they
were smart
enough to follow
the radical, for
that's usually the
most conservative
way to go.

Tree Hugger

After my love
hugs a tree
I hug her
and she smells
half like a tree
and half like
a human
and that is
her essence—
half-human
half-tree.
They are not
so different from
one another,
human and tree.
Both sway
in the wind.
Both can stand
reasonably still.
And don't forget
more than once
a tree, trying
to escape from
other trees, turned
into a human.
But they are
never happy in
in their new
human form

even though
they got away.

The Palace of Wisdom

leads to the road
of excess, eight-inch heels
excess, pink, almost leather,
beyond the knee, so add eight
inches to the human's height,
that's all the shop, the palace,
sells, open-toe, closed-toe,
rhinestones, laced, unlaced,
all the laced varieties with
practical side zippers.
The owner does all her pole
work at a women-only studio
with no mirrors, shadowy
and sultry music,
reclaiming the female
body, exuberance, and
sexuality, free of the male touch
and gaze. She keeps the store
open late on nights the local
strip clubs are open on Broadway
so if the women who work those
strip and pole clubs have a shoe
emergency they can run over or
send a messenger or beg for
a delivery. Those clubs full
of male gazes, and touches.
I was always frightened of
eight inch heels and genital
coverings with just a suggestion

of materials. I can't go to the
women only studio and I'm sure
I shouldn't go to the local clubs.
My love is buying two pair of
eight-inch heels, pink calf high,
and black thigh high, with
laces. They can't be stacked
so eight more inches is all
she'll get. I loved watching her
try on both pairs and confer
at length with the proprietor,
carefully, with reverence,
and though she doesn't dwell
much in front of mirrors,
she did so tonight.
And I loved watching her take
them off. And in the middle
of it all a woman called from
one of the clubs. She needed
new shoes and press on nails
and we volunteered to drop
them off. My love wanted to
do it to be nice and I wanted to
do it to be nice and to go inside.
But did my love want to go
inside as well? The proprietor
didn't take us up on our offer.
We walked home carrying
the heavy bag between us

with the two pair of boots
and one black lace bodysuit,
one loop of the bag in
each of our hands.
The owner locked up and
rushed out with us to make
the special delivery.
The dancer's heel had broken
and another show was
about to begin. I got
my own show back home.
I wasn't embarrassed at all.
I loved every second.

The Hummingbird's Tongue

Today I saw a hummingbird's tongue
for the first time, its glistening thread
darting out of the glistening thread
of its beak. And when I remarked,
you who thinks the best of me,
of people, said I was mistaken
and I had seen this tongue before.
You said hummingbird's are never
still and I say, like every object
in the universe, always trying to
impress you with my astrophysics,
but you know when to ignore me,
thank god.

To Textile Manufacturers

The ideal underwear
should have two panels,
the front panel should do
a pretty good job covering
the genitals and the rear
panel, larger than the front,
should do not as good
a job covering the buttocks
and these two panels should
be connected with a slender
ribbon which has a slight
gleam, as a ribbon around
a wrapped present may have,
and the panels themselves
should be of the softest
thinnest cotton, if not prewashed
a thousand times before
leaving the plant, at least
the illusion of that process.
And keep the tag to a minimum,
and silky. I won't give advice
as to color and pattern but be
guided by the principle that
they should not overwhelm
the basic design which is classic
in its delicacy, beauty and ratio
of concealment and revealment
and gives the wearer great
pleasure pulling them up the legs

and a hint of regret sliding them
down, and if there is another in
proximity, helping, even though
they may be overwhelmed with
the desire to pull those underwear
off, they may also have
a hint of regret.

Bad Timing

For the first time in 61 years one of our
children walked in at the wrong time,
and none of us had a heart attack,
parents or child, no lightning
struck. We laughed a laugh we never
laughed before, amazingly only
slightly embarrassed. And it wasn't
the very wrong time, it was just after
the time that could have really been
the very wrong time.

When I Return

I've never told you this, or anyone else,
and so I'll tell the world that does not
listen. When I return from a night
and morning of lovemaking with you
I can do nothing more than wander
about my house for two or three hours,
maybe looking out the window at the
light, maybe sweeping what was
already swept, maybe laying down
to try to nap, nothing more, and I
was always ashamed of my laziness,
and now I realize I should have been
proud I was simply trying to keep
my composure, and to do all I could
do in those precious moments.

It All Feels Good

You're asleep, or somewhere between
99 and 100 percent, leg bent up
towards me, an invitation? We're both
breathing but there is no sound of
breath. I hold your ankle
firmly and my crotch/cock rests
against your foot, lightly, and then over
minutes, many minutes, I gradually
harden, and I wonder if in your
99–100 world you feel it and then
I'm hard, harder than I've ever been,
and then over minutes,
many minutes, I soften, back to
resting state and fall asleep.

The Most Peaceful Day

If I tell you I am having
the most peaceful day
I've ever had I fear
you'd say I am prone
to exaggerate and one
shouldn't rank or compare
days anyway. And that I am
just trying to torture
myself into worrying
that I won't have
another day like this.
And our impending
debate will be part of
the peaceful pleasure.

My Higher Self

I have always hated
that I couldn't possess you
and then for a split second
I reveled in your wild,
anarchic, mysterious life.

Doing the Dishes

At first I did your dishes
not to keep my hands warm
or to feel the clean plates
or to avoid conversation
but to woo you and then I learned
you were never happy with
the results, nor how much
water I used for those results,
that there was always remains
of the last meal, and then I
did your dishes to bother you.
And now it's just that I like
to do the dishes and perhaps
teach you a small lesson,
that it's best not to let them
accumulate but to do them
after every meal, except
those times in life
when that's impossible.

With My Love After the Symphony

If we were in our early sixties then she
was in her late seventies. We met
on the 49 bus after MTT, with a brain
tumor, came out of retirement to conduct
the 9th and accidentally threw his baton
which grazed the eyebrow of the third
violinist in the row of 1st violins and she
violated the strict time immemorial
prohibition against smiling and smiled
albeit briefly and the woman we met
on the bus hadn't seen the throw
as she was either looking away
from MTT and/or was sitting higher up
so the projectile was lost to her.
She herself was very small, Asian with a
long blue wool coat and black leather shoes
and her eyebrows had been patiently
worked to the thinnest of crescents.
We talked easily, she and the two of us,
laughing and appreciating being alive
though never of course saying we were
appreciating being alive and in the great
rush of thoughts I had pleasant day dreams
of the three of us being naked together
for I am not one who exclusively dreams
of being with younger lovers, and that
was that, and then months later
on the same bus or at least a different
bus with the same number because one

can never enter the same bus twice
we met the same woman after the same
or at least similar symphony orchestra
played the nutcracker. There is no
greater music than the cliches of
classical music, this one reinvigorated
with the accompaniment of an
acrobat troupe, including someone
who climbed up and down a ladder
which was not leaning on anything other
than air. It wasn't MTT but a vigorous
young man conducting and he didn't
sit down or lose his baton once
all evening and our conversation
was delightful again and in the rush
of thoughts I had the same dream as
the first time, one track mind, one trick
pony, I guess, and whether it was just
preternatural shyness, diffidence,
circumspection, or all of the above
simply being fancy words,
psychoanalytic words for fear of
rejection, shyness, humiliation and
embarrassment, I initiated no inquiries
related to that special thought and she
got off at Jackson Street and we stayed
on to Union and I had that recurring
regret, not again, not again, though
with a faint smile, as I was getting off

at Union with the love of my life,
no small matter, and I remembered I
had promised to give my youngest son
advice every day now that we are far
away from each other and today's
advice is *don't be afraid to ask, no
matter what,* but I know I can be
a schmuck, so I have to be careful,
my son, on the other hand, is a sweet
and kind young man so he should not
be afraid of any reply. My love, who
never heard the 9th or gave it a thought
was still buzzing more deeply with
its majesty than I ever would, and
she'll make a joke about my shyness
on the bus, claiming I'm not shy at all.

Trophy

It took my love twenty minutes
to describe the animal tracks
she found deep in the forest.
She used her nuanced words
and her left hand as a visual aid,
as if her fingers were holding
a precious gem up to show off.
There was the segment about
the depth and circumference.
The segment about the pads,
both number and shape.
And the segment about one
track in particular that, due to
the shallower depth and firmness
of the snow, revealed the kind
of fur that wrapped over the pad,
all leading to her conclusion
that it was not a mountain lion
or coyote but a lynx, and the
lynx, according to authorities,
are long gone from that forest,
and so, the forest service, or
the forest disservice, which was
planning to harvest trees there
can no longer do so, because
it is lynx habitat. Everything
is political, inadvertently, or not.
I, hearing the lecture, dreamed
not of the tracks but of the lynx

in the air, between tracks and
how little time its paws touch
the earth as it dashes through
the forest, and how much time
it's suspended in the air, in
flight. But she wasn't finished
yet, there was an epilogue with
a snow shoe hare, at least with one
paw she found in a pool of fresh
blood, along with a neat pile
of intestines, in a scuffle area
in the middle of the tracks,
which resumed a little heavier
in the snow on the far
side of the scuffle, as the
lynx was then running with its
trophy shaking in its mouth.

Smell

When you said oh my god I love your smell
I was so happy you finally loved my smell
but then I realized it was you you were
smelling on me and that made me laugh
and be even happier.

Osha

And speaking of
healing fragrance
you said Osha
proliferated
during covid.
At first I balked
at this theory.
Second, I
praised you.
Third, I
believed you.

X

On and Off

Powdery blue thigh high
stockings draped over
the 200-year-old East Lake
Victorian chair my mother
cherished, the stockings are
still partly rolled at the
top, inducing a priapistic
condition and echoing
the swirling spiral pattern
that is everywhere in
nature and the memory
of them rolling down
your legs either by accident
or the aid of your hands,
all of which is a forgettable
preamble to what I simply
wanted to say—
on and off and on and off.
There are important
particulars that accompany
these words but no one will
know what they are except
for you, everyone else will
simply wonder or tell their
own story, or yawn, on
and off and on and off.
The stockings are slightly
soiled, which is far preferable

to them being completely
clean or very soiled and even
the old chair is crying out
in joy and gratitude for
being given the honor of
holding them up for display.

Time Constraints

Because of time constraints
I only laid out three outfits
for you for my pleasure.

Hierarchy

Even if there was no hierarchy,
even if we don't believe in hierarchy,
you are and can only ever be No. 1.

Makeup

Our city's enemies say it's in a
death spiral, and I won't argue,
but I did see, today, 30 women
in a makeup shop, in the
most troubled neighborhood, roaming
from station to station, each painting
a sample of lipstick, gloss, paint, eye
shadow, glitter, on the back
of their left hands, for as luck will have it
they were all righties, so their hands
were like rainbows, or artists' pallets,
which leads to the conclusion that the
pallets themselves are works of art.
I have never seen such a group
of divine, unhumorous, joyfully serious
people, with deep concentration, deep
attention to detail, deep respect for
color theory, and indeed, the deep
principle that art itself is meant not
only for the creator but for the audience,
the viewers. I should mention that I
am an old man and in love for the first
time and my love has told me a thousand
times, with deep sincerity, that she
loves me but I love her so much
I'm afraid I'll lose her and I'm also, truth
be told, enflamed for everyone here.
It's my first time in a makeup shop,
and if I wasn't in love I wouldn't be

dreaming of everyone else dabbing,
spritzing and pasting samples.
I wish everyone in the world
could join me now. The greatest artists
devote themselves to art they
know won't last long enough to be
remembered by anyone, but I'll
remember all of these artists, my love
most especially, though at this time
I barely exist for her, she is so
rapt and serious a creator.

Calling Names

For half a decade I worried about calling
you my ex-wife's name and now that you
called me your ex-husband's name
I don't have to worry about it anymore
and I can complain to you endlessly
about calling me his name, and it
wasn't just his name but his
endearing nickname!

Wishbone

My mother was kind to plants,
animals and people. On Friday
nights she'd clean the wishbone
and set it aside so it could dry
overnight and crack easily
in the morning after we
both made our silent wishes.
I only remember this sixty
ears later when you presented
a double plum, the two had
grown together and looked
like a male ball sack, only
deep purple, nearly translucent.
We both pulled at once and it
seemed like the plums we each
came away with were the same
size so both our wishes will
come true. I winced all those
years ago when I felt and heard
the bone crack, using the late
animal for our superstitious
pleasure. I wonder if my mother
winced as well, she was more
sensitive than I am. How rarely
we talk about our illustrious
mothers. We didn't wince at all
when the plums came apart
and when we kissed after biting
into our plums the juices of

the two joined together again
in our mouths. I wonder if our
wishes were for each other.

My Love

slides my hot hand off her,
it's hot because I am hot for her
and she's already too hot
from a hot flash so I roll away
and write this which I don't finish
because the hot flash is over
and she is no longer repelled
by my heat. Our arms wrap
around each other like bands
around two barrels stored at
a now perfect temperature.
We hear, outside and below,
the great weight of the first
bus of the day, empty at 5:22
in the morning as it rolls over
the steel plate in the street,
the rubber wheels pound the plate
into its temporary asphalt housing
and it sounds like a heavy wooden
door closing in its perfectly fitted frame,
the door in the priest's house
in Choquerkirao (never conquered)
where a group of contemporary historians
now claim the Incas didn't practice
human child sacrifice, they merely loved
and love, mother earth. It was my master
who told me to start one place and
end another and so our bed today
and Peru 500 years ago. I won't mention

my master's name because it is already
vanishing after the great fame he received
in his lifetime. I suppose he'd be happy
the jungle of time is already covering it up.

Of the Americas

I love how Avenue of the Americas
is Avenue of the Americas
and not of America. May Americas
be no accident and always be so.
On its wide sidewalk today
I appreciated sexy clothing
for the first time, and when your
white stockings, visibly topping
out just under the bottom of your
beaded dress, accidently rolled
down your legs, like a flag sliding
down a pole, first the left flag
then the right, no more countries,
and the rolls caught in your leather
boots, just below the tops, I
imagined pulling off your boots
and then the white nylon stockings,
slowly, for one should rarely
rush the process towards
nakedness with a loved one.
Your calves, ankles and feet all
hot from stewing in the cauldrons
of your boots. Is the owner of all
of it, that's you, the witch stirring
the cauldron? Somebody
found a four-hundred-year-old
stirring spoon and gave it to you,
but not before they stopped to
imagine the lives surrounding

that spoon, so long ago, all full
of desire, as I am, dreaming of
when we leave this beautiful
avenue and find some privacy.

Happy Birthday!

Your birthday and your back was to me
and you weren't moving much and I was
moving a lot and it all happened quickly,
for me, I even tried to stop it from happening,
instead of the usual encouraging it and since
it was your birthday and I know my
quietness and gentleness in lovemaking
bothers you, since it's your birthday
I said (to myself) why not and I let
out a sky is falling scream, which
I'm still hoarse from, and you
laughed, and asked, while I was
still in you, if I was faking it,
and I said of course, and that
it was also the most natural thing
in the world and I was the most
serious man in the world.
I was a coyote howling at night,
I don't know if you understood
my double answer, but you did
thank me for giving you
so much pleasure while you lay
still. Happy birthday!

Breakfast

For
the
first
time
I
waited
until
I
was
out
of
you
to
ask
what
was
for
breakfast.

Yawn

When you yawned in the beginning
of lovemaking I thought that's ok,
it's not going to work, and I thought
what the hell, it might work anyway,
and it worked, anyway.

The Right Mirror

At the DeYoung fashion exhibit
you were interested in who wore
the dresses and where they
were worn whereas I was merely
imagining you in every dress,
and then imagining the dress
crumpled beside you.
There were mirrors everywhere
and believe it or not a docent
told me if I don't like my smile
I should find a better mirror.
A woman named "Dodie" wore
the most outrageously beautiful
dresses to the most rarified
galas, and then gave them to
the museum, including a jacket
that was a tulip, red, without
arm holes so the jacket doubled
as a silk straight jacket. Often
the dresses were too much
or too little but every now and then
a perfect tulip made it all the
way from Amsterdam. You who
usually dress so simply
were enthralled. I found the
right mirror fifty years ago,
over my mother's desk.
It was very old and mottled
with curdling mercury and

peeling skin. I had to tilt
my head to get most
of my face to show,
that in itself made
me laugh. I wonder who
is enjoying that mirror now.
We're hiding in our respective
bathrooms, waiting for closing
time to come out and then
each will try on everything,
regardless of gender.
I wonder if we'll leave
all the outfits crumpled
beside the naked manikins,
or if we'll patiently
redress the cold statues.

True Love

Somehow, even though I am riven
by jealousy, self-doubts and a deep
fear of true love and its terrible
power to make cataclysmic changes
to one's very essence, and so
I never wanted to see you again,
I forgot all that as I spent the
afternoon of your return in great
joy, perhaps the greatest joy of
my life, collecting broken seashells
for you, three small polished swirls
from Chrissy Beach, getting your
altered jacket at the tailor,
your dry cleaning, shopping
for blueberries, onions,
all of your favorites, and lastly,
stopping at Patricia's,
the sidewalk florist, for a bouquet,
where a beautiful young woman
in front of me said Patricia's
flowers are the best in the city
and she (the young woman) picks
one flower first for Patricia to
surround with a bouquet, today
a blue rose, and she made a rare
additional request for lavender
because the bouquet was for her
mother who loves lavender,
I told her my bouquet was for

my love who I was about to pick up
at the airport and she asked if
I was bringing the bouquet with me
to greet my love and with a pang
of failed romanticism I said no
because we were going to the
ballet and I didn't want the flowers
to wilt in the car and she asked
me if it was Swan Lake, no, I said,
Midsummer's Night's dream, good,
she said, Swan Lake is overdone.
I told her I let Patricia do all the
arranging without any advice,
I don't even suggest one flower
to start and she said she had two
espresso martinis already
so even the trolley cars
look beautiful. I didn't tell her
I just saw DijonStreak on
Columbus with blue flannel
pants waiting for the
street poet with the manual
typewriter to type him a poem,
Dijon, a 90-year-old crooner
and punk rock lover and
I didn't tell Patricia I've written
more than one poem about her,
rationalizing it's best to keep some secrets.
Patricia told me Pajara en Cama

means see you tomorrow in Quichua.
She was playing Tania Libertad
on her box and complained to me
about another person who asked
for the price of a bouquet then put
it down and rushed away. People
are moving too quickly these days,
she said, and I thought, that's me
but I kept that secret as well.
The ranunculo or ranunculus
has more silky layers than the
finest croissant. I broke with
tradition and asked Patricia
for five sunflowers and one
ranunculo, a second bouquet.
I always left it in her hands until
I requested the five and one,
because I know you love sunflowers
and I wanted to show off I knew
the name ranunculo. I'm sure
Patricia grumbled the yellow
and white was an aesthetic stretch.
The two bouquets under one arm
were like a barrel, the dry cleaning
under the other arm, and the pack
of food on my back, and a happiness
I never felt before, as if I'm walking
around in this world for you, and,
somehow I had the crazy certainty

you felt the same about me and
knowing that was just a part
of my joy.

x

Silk Bag

The stockings are yours, all yours,
so why, whenever I leave, do I
slip them into my little slip string
silk bag and carry them away
with me, and I do it always when
you are turned away, but I don't
believe you don't notice they are
gone, but you don't say anything,
discretion or not knowing what
to say, I don't know. They are
curious tokens for me, of love,
fulfilled and unfulfilled, as all
great loves are.

A Great Hula Hooper

Thumb on clit,
index and middle
finger inside,
pinky and ring finger
on anus, all circling
at once, like a great
hula hooper with many
hoops spinning around
her waist.

Ridicule

Both of us up in the middle
of the night, I caress you
from your neck down to
and below your buttocks,
and you say *are you serious
or are you just patting my ass?*
I say *if you can't tell then get
the hell out of here,* dripping
with ridicule, but mostly
kidding. Then we hug before
you get up for a snack
and I answer your question
that I'm not really sure.
A serious answer, even though
I was really sure. And then I
remembered it was your house
so you probably won't get the
hell out, but send me on my
way, instead.

Go Low

I love it when you go low.
When I slide my hand down
between your pants
and your buttocks,
and I completely
give over to despair that
it's just pants and skin,
and then, when I'm sure
there is nothing else,
so very low down,
I am thrilled to find
the frayed cotton band
of your underwear.

Lies

I told you I found a small sack
of boletes and caught a catfish
and took them home and fried
them in garlic and butter
and you knew I was lying
about the catfish but telling
the truth about the boletes
garlic and butter, but didn't
even call me out on it, you
just said "nice." I love how
you always know when I
am lying and when I am
telling the truth, but it
also infuriates me.

Alarming

How alarming it was when our
new lover told us she left her
husband because he shamed her
when she said she wanted to
open up their marriage. Alarming
because although we are open,
every time you're with another,
I shame you and then say
I didn't mean to, but can
shaming ever be by accident?
I don't think so.

Cool Hands

I don't wear gloves
and I keep my hands apart
before I touch you
so they don't make
each other hot
and you don't recoil
from my heat.

Glitter and Ashes

I didn't know you were on all fours
looking for a small jar of glitter
mixed with your friend's ashes
so I touched you and started
to pull your pants down and you
weren't offended. And now
it's time to hear your friend's story.

Uncovering

Just a mound of needles
and loam and you scooped
it away like the most careful
paleontologist and there
it was, the most perfect
bolete in the history
of boletes.

Kept Ribbon

The priest gave you
a St. Francis medallion
with a small blue ribbon.
You touched it as if it was
toxic and gave it to me
because you believe
the gift of a gift makes
all the difference in the
world, it cleanses any
sin away. I placed the
medallion in a jade tree
but I kept the ribbon
for my drawer of remnants.

Balm Jar

I am an expert lover so I opened
and closed your balm jar with
only one hand while keeping the other
hand on you and you said what
I was afraid you'd say *don't close it
I may need more* but I had already
closed it so I reopened it and then
you didn't need anymore but
don't worry these thoughts only
occurred to me afterwards
I was completely in the moment
with you at the time, at least
almost completely in the moment.

Shook

I love how you shook your underwear
off your second foot with two gentle kicks,
the first not quite a success and the
second a great one.

Preparing

I love preparing to see other lovers,
together with you, you shaving
carefully and filling up your kink bag,
and me washing obsessively and
talking of other things, just the two of us,
together, before we go our separate ways.

Bodies

The way people who can control their bodies
shift from one side to the other, by instinct,
when they are laying down, you did that,
and your hand that was draped over
my chest slid across me at an intermediate
speed, except at the end, at the edge
of my chest it changed to a slow speed
so the last inch or so took longer to cross
than the whole rest of the slide,
like slowing at the end when pulling
down a shade. And I don't know
if it was reluctance to leave my body,
or else a kind of teasing, but I do know,
if I asked you, you'd give your stock
answer of *both* to my either/or question,
but I'll ask you now anyway, just to
hear your answer.

The Order of Oral Sex

Because I usually go down
on you first I think it must
be sexist and patriarchal
but then I read an expert
who said the opposite is true,
so I don't know if it's so,
and today you went down
on me first and since I'm
just a man, before I could
go down on you I fell
half asleep and noticed
you started messaging
another lover, I thought,
since I wasn't doing my job,
and that woke me up
enough to get to work,
or I should say get to pleasure,
and you stopped messaging
but I thought it would be
ok if you continued, while
I was doing what I, indeed,
love to do for you, even if
I occasionally fall asleep
on the job.

Seven Beaches in a Day

Walking seven beaches
in the mist with you,
a feat not done every
day. I was glad that you
would have an amazing
story to tell when you
see your other lovers
later; the hard walk,
all the big ups and
downs, the sludge
of fog, the banana
slug migration, and
the world's largest
camera obscura.

Branch

You leaned a branch against a tree
near the edge of the forest and said we'll
look for that as a landmark on the way
back, and I thought of that branch the
whole way in. But I knew I shouldn't worry
that we'd never find that leaning
branch in such a vast forest, because
I also knew we'd find our way home,
one way or another, together.

About the Author

Peter Waldor is the author of twenty-nine books of poetry, including *Who Touches Everything,* which won the National Jewish Book Award for poetry. He is also the author of a book of essays, *Seven Quilts*. His book *Gate Posts With No Gate* is a poetry-art collaboration with a group of visual artists. He was the 2014–2015 Poet Laureate of San Miguel County, Colorado. His poetry has appeared widely in magazines, including *Ploughshares, American Poetry Review, The Colorado Review, Fungi Magazine,* and *Mothering Magazine*. He lives in Ophir, Colorado.

www.ingramcontent.com/pod-product-compliance
Lightning Source LLC
Chambersburg PA
CBHW031203160426
43193CB00008B/480